Contents

The First People of New York

The first people of New York were Native Americans. They were hunters and **foragers**, people who moved from place to place in search of food. They arrived in the region about 14,000 to 13,000 years ago from the south and west. **Descendants** of these people are called the Algonquians after the languages that they spoke. By the time Europeans arrived in what is now New York, the Algonquians included many different groups, or tribes, such as the Montauks, Raritans, Tappans, Wappingers, Esopus, and Mahicans. The Algonquian tribes lived near waterways where they could fish and hunt, and travel in their canoes. There were Algonquians near Lake Champlain and Lake George, as well as in the Hudson River valley and along the **coast** of Long Island.

About 1,000 years before the Europeans arrived, another Native American group moved into the area. Known as the Iroquois, they were made up of five tribes. These tribes were the Onondagas, Senecas, Cayugas, Oneidas, and Mohawks. These five tribes were said to fight among themselves. To stop this fighting, they formed the Iroquois Confederacy. Each of the five nations had its own leader and governed itself, but they would all cooperate in times of need.

New York's
European Explorers

Daniel R. Faust and Amelie von Zumbusch

PowerKiDS press.

New York

Published in 2015 by The Rosen Publishing Group, Inc.
29 East 21st Street, New York, NY 10010

Book Design: Chris Brand

Photo Credits: Cover (Henry Hudson), (Christopher Colombus), pp. 5, 11 Stock Montage/Archive Photos/Getty Images; cover (Samuel De Champlain) Leemage/ Universal Images Group/Getty Images; p. 7 Anonymous/The Bridgeman Art Library/ Getty Images; pp. 9, 13 (inset), 13 © Hulton/Archive; p. 15 Hemera Technologies/ Photos.com/Thinkstock; p. 15 (inset) English School/The Bridgeman Art Library/ Getty Images; p. 17 Don Emmert/AFP/Getty Images; p. 19 (inset) © Museum of the City of New York; p. 19 © Collection of the New-York Historical Society; p. 21 (left inset) iStock/Thinkstock; p. 21 (right inset) Amy Riley/E+/Getty Images; p. 21 Adam Jones/Photo Researcher/Getty Images.

Library of Congress Cataloging-in-Publication Data

Faust, Daniel R.
New York's European explorers / by Daniel R. Faust and Amelie von Zumbusch.
p. cm. — (Spotlight on New York)
Includes index.
ISBN 978-1-4777-7341-3 (pbk.)
ISBN 978-1-4777-7289-8 (6-pack)
ISBN 978-1-4777-7320-8 (library binding)
1. New York (State) — Discovery and exploration — Juvenile literature. 2. Explorers — New York (State) — History — Juvenile literature. 3. New York (State) — History — Colonial period, ca. 1600-1775 — Juvenile literature. I. Faust, Daniel R. II. Zumbusch, Amelie von. III. Title.
F122.F38 2015
974.7—d23

Manufactured in the United States of America

CPSIA Compliance Information: Batch #WS15RC: For further information contact Rosen Publishing, New York, New York at 1-800-237-9932.

This illustration shows an artist's representation of what an Iroquois village in New York State might have looked like before Europeans came to North America.

Explorers Look for New Lands

Starting in the mid-1400s, European rulers began to fund the journeys of **explorers**. Explorers are people who travel to new places to learn about them. Many of the European explorers from this period were looking for a **water route** to the riches of Asia.

The European rulers wanted to play a bigger role in the **profitable** trade with Asia. At the time, the goods that reached Europe from Asia, such as silk and spices, were brought overland. People in Asia and the Middle East controlled most stages of the trade. The European rulers also hoped that the explorers they backed would find new lands from which they could get valuable **natural resources**, such as silver and gold.

Some explorers headed south around the tip of Africa. Others believed that there was a faster way to reach Asia by sailing west across the Atlantic Ocean. When they attempted to do so, they discovered North and South America lay in between!

This is a painting of Henry the Navigator, a Portuguese prince who backed many of the explorers who played an important role in the early days of what became known as the Age of Exploration.

7

Exploring North and South America

The first of the European explorers from this period to reach the Americas was Christopher Columbus. Ferdinand and Isabella, the rulers of Spain, funded his **expedition**. It had three ships, the *Niña*, the *Pinta*, and the *Santa María*. The expedition first caught sight of North American land on October 12, 1492. Columbus landed on an island that he named San Salvador. He thought this island was near the East Indies, which is what Europeans called Southeast Asia. However, he was wrong. It was really in what we now call the Bahamas, a couple of hundred miles off the coast of what is now Florida.

Many other European explorers followed Columbus. In 1499, an Italian explorer named Amerigo Vespucci, invited by the king of Portugal, explored the northern coast of Brazil, in South America. Vespucci was likely the first person to suggest that the lands he and Columbus had explored were not part of Asia. The name "America" comes from Vespucci's first name.

In 1494, a letter that Christopher Columbus had written about his journey was published in a book commonly called *On the Recently Discovered Islands in the Indian Sea*. This picture shows Columbus's ship among the islands he explored. Columbus didn't make any maps of the places he visited, so the artist had to use his imagination to make the picture.

num copia ſalubritate admixta bominū : quæ niſi
quis viderit : credulitatem ſuperat . Huius arbores
paſcua & fructus / multū ab illis Iohanę differūt .
Hæc præterea Hiſpana diuerſo aromatis genere /
auro metalliſcꝫ abundat. cuius quidem & omnium
aliarum quas ego vidi : & quarum cognitionem
ɧabeo incolę vtriuſcꝫ ſexus : nudi ſemꝑ incedunt :

Native Americans Meet European Explorers

In 1497, the Italian explorer Giovanni Caboto, known as John Cabot in English, sailed along the northern Atlantic coast of North America. The king of England funded his expedition. Though Cabot likely only sailed as far south as Newfoundland, in Canada, the English would later claim the land that is New York based on this expedition.

An Italian named Giovanni da Verrazzano, sailing for the French king, explored the eastern coast of America in 1524. He wrote in his journal that the Native Americans were very friendly. They even showed him the safest places to land his ship. In 1534, a French explorer named Jacques Cartier landed in what is now Canada. The Algonquian and Iroquoian people who lived there greeted him kindly.

In spite of the warm welcome, explorers and the **colonists** who followed did not always treat the Native Americans well. They sometimes took Native Americans by force and brought them back to Europe. Native Americans learned that they could not always trust the explorers. To protect themselves, they sometimes attacked the Europeans.

This image shows a nineteenth-century artist's idea of what French explorer Jacques Cartier may have looked like. There are no portraits of Cartier that date from the time in which he lived.

11

An Italian Explorer: Giovanni da Verrazzano

      Italian explorer Giovanni da Verrazzano was chosen by King Francis I of France to lead an expedition in 1524. Verrazzano was trying to find the Northwest Passage, a way to reach Asia by sailing through North America. He brought along his brother Girolamo, who was a **cartographer**. He made maps of the lands they found on their journey.

      Verrazzano landed on the Atlantic coast in the area that is now North Carolina. He sailed south for over 100 miles before turning around and heading back north. He entered New York Harbor and sailed along the coast of what we now call Long Island. He was impressed with all of the beautiful plants growing there. He named that area Flora after the ancient Roman goddess of flowers. Girolamo da Verrazzano drew Long Island on the map he made. Soon most of Europe knew about the newly discovered island.

This map of the New World is part of a larger world map made by Girolamo da Verrazzano, in about 1529. The picture of Giovanni da Verrazzano was made long after his death. The writing at the bottom of the picture gives his name and says that he is the discoverer of New France, the name given to the lands he claimed for France in the New World.

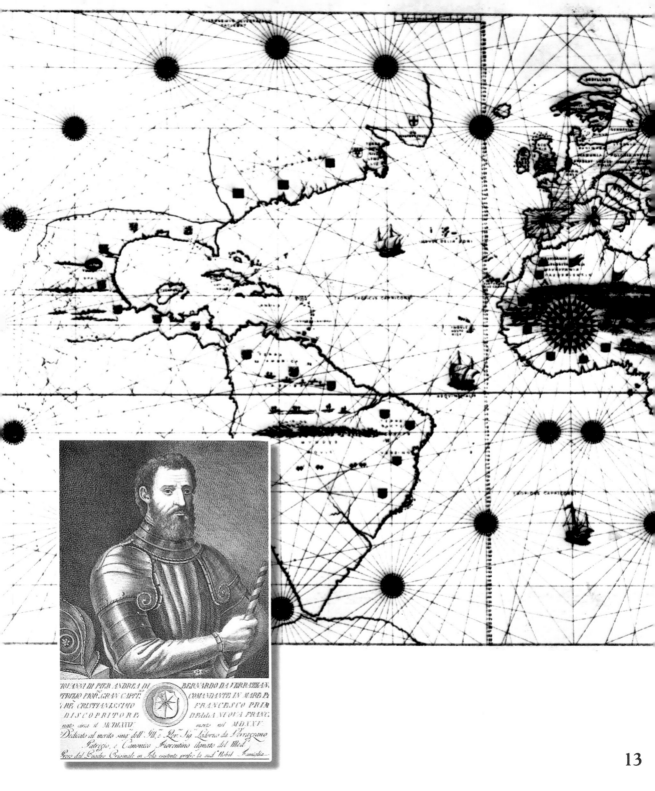

13

A French Explorer: Samuel de Champlain

Samuel de Champlain was an explorer, cartographer, and the founder of New France, which later became Canada. In 1603, Champlain led his first expedition to what is now Canada. Two years later, he sailed along the coast of what is now New England. He also explored parts of northern New York, such as the lake that was later named Lake Champlain.

Champlain's expeditions were part of France's desire to establish a colony in North America. The French wanted North America's natural resources, particularly the fur of its beavers, which had become rare in Europe. The French presence resulted in rivalry between the Dutch, English, and French over the Hudson River valley and its access to the Great Lakes and the continent's interior that would last until the English captured French Canada.

Champlain built a fort at what is now called Quebec City, in Canada. He tried to establish good relations with the Native Americans who lived in the area, like the Hurons and the Algonquins. These natives asked the French for help in their conflict with the powerful Iroquois tribes of what is now New York. This first **interaction** between the French and the Iroquois, a battle on the shore of Lake Champlain, would set the tone for the poor relations between the two groups for the next hundred years.

This statue of Samuel de Champlain stands in Ottawa, the capital of modern-day Canada. The round object in the statue's hand is a mariner's astrolabe, a device used by sailors and explorers to navigate while at sea.

An English Explorer: Henry Hudson

English explorer Henry Hudson was hired by Dutch **merchants** in 1609 to find a sea route through the Northwest Passage to the East Indies. Unlike Verrazzano and Champlain, he tried to sail around the North Pole. When that didn't work, Hudson sailed his ship, the *Half Moon*, south, along the coast of North America. In time, he reached what is now New York Harbor. Then he sailed north, up the large river that flowed into the harbor. The river is named the Hudson River after Henry Hudson.

Hudson hoped this river would lead to the Pacific Ocean and then to the East Indies. It did not. However, based upon Hudson's reports, the Dutch decided to charter companies to establish **trading posts** in North America. In 1624, the Dutch sent **settlers** to what would become New Netherland.

In 1610, the English hired Hudson to lead an expedition into Canada. Hudson's ship became trapped in ice and, as their supplies ran low, his crew became unhappy. Hudson's crew took over the ship. They set Hudson, along with several others, **adrift** in a small boat. They were never seen again.

> Hudson's ship, the *Half Moon*, was 85 feet long and carried a crew of twenty men. A copy of the ship was built in 1989 and is operated by the New Netherland Museum. Visitors can sail up and down the Hudson River on it!

A Dutch Explorer: Adriaen Block

The Dutch sent explorer Adriaen Block to discover possible places to establish trading posts in the Hudson River region. In January 1614, before Block could return to Holland, one of his two ships was destroyed by fire. Block and his crew lived on Manhattan Island while they built a new ship. In the spring of 1614, Block and his crew sailed for home. They sailed around a large island that Block named Lange Eylandt, or Long Island. This was the same island that Verrazzano had named Flora 70 years earlier. Block explored Long Island Sound and the Connecticut River. Block Island, which is 14 miles east of Long Island, was named after Adriaen Block.

Block drew up a map of the areas he explored when he returned home to the Netherlands. His map was the first to use the name "New Netherland" for the land between English Virginia and French Canada. News of these lands spread as people learned about Block's **voyage** and his map.

Block called the land he explored New Netherland. He made a chart of the area during his expedition of 1613–1614. A part of the chart is shown here. The small picture shows New Netherland's official seal. Beaver fur was so important to Dutch colonists and traders that they put a picture of a beaver on the seal. The beads around the beaver are wampum beads.

NEDERLANDT

IROQOISIA

ALMOUCHICOISEN

MAHICANS. MAKIMANES.

SEQVINS

MORHICANS

PEQVATS.

NAWAAS

NAPAANOOS

QVAMACHKES

NAHICANS

Sywanois.

Wijte Bay

De Gebroken Hoeck

De vlacke hoeck

SIGILLVM • NOVI • BELGII •

Duytsche Mijlen Tot 15 voor een Graedt

New York's Many Riches

When the Native Americans first arrived in the area that would become New York, they found an area that was rich in natural resources. Rivers and lakes contained an abundance of fish, and the woodlands were home to animals that could be used for food and clothing. Native Americans used dyed porcupine quills and small shells to decorate their clothing. About the time that Europeans arrived, they began using clam and whelk shells to make beads called **wampum**. Soon wampum was used as **currency** in their trade with Europeans and to make belts that helped them remember important events.

Dutch traders were among the first Europeans to establish businesses in North America, by building trading posts along the Hudson River. They quickly learned that they could get animal furs from the Native Americans in **exchange** for metal tools, guns, blankets, clothing, and other goods. Traders could sell these furs in Europe for high prices. Soon farmers arrived. The food they produced supported the traders and merchants in the growing settlements.

Native Americans used the bark from trees, like the elm, to make their canoes and homes. Clam and whelk shells were used to make beads. These beads were used to decorate clothing and to make wampum. The Native American fur trade attracted the attention of Dutch, English, and French merchants. Beaver fur, for example, could be sold in Europe for a lot of money.

Beaver

Quahogs

American Elm

After the Explorers Came the Colonists

The area that became New York and the lives of the Native Americans living there changed forever after the European explorers arrived. The maps and reports the explorers brought back made Europeans want to move to the new lands. At first, just a few people moved. By the early 1600s, countries in Europe were creating permanent colonies in North America. However, the land that the Europeans settled was already occupied by Native Americans.

Encounters between European colonists and Native Americans were not always peaceful. The growth of European colonies often caused conflicts with Indian people, who sometimes were forced from their lands. Although Indians wanted to keep their lands, wars with colonists and other Indians, and the loss of their people from diseases brought by Europeans, made this difficult. Some native people sold their land to the settlers. Others became Christians and lived near the settlements of missionaries.

The colonists came from many countries, including the Netherlands, England, and France. They brought with them tools, foods, and **traditions** from their homelands. They helped to create the New York we live in today.